UNTIL THE
BLUE
KINGDOM
COMES

Sept. 12, 2011

to Sandy,

May your life be filled
with the blessings of
poetry and the poetry
of blessings!

15/3/3/81

Jim

UNTIL THE BLUE KINGDOM COMES

POEMS

JAMES B. ROSENBERG

Cover Art by Elise Luce Kraemer

Library of Congress Control Number: 2010919260
ISBN: Softcover   978-1-4568-0837-2
               Ebook   978-1-4568-0838-9

The following poems have previously appeared in the *CCAR JOURNAL:
THE REFORM JEWISH QUARTERLY*: "The Gift of Silence,"
"*Modeh Ani Lifanecha,*" "You!," "Nightmare," "Final Journey."

"The Gift of Silence" and "Bitter Lemon" have previously appeared in
THE RHODE ISLAND WRITERS' CIRCLE ANTHOLOGY 2008,
Providence, R.I., The Poet's Press.

To order additional copies of this book, contact:
Xlibris Corporation
1-888-795-4274
www.Xlibris.com
Orders@Xlibris.com
88035

CONTENTS

I. Sing aloud for the coming of the light!

II. The White Cliffs Beckon Still.

III. Blue, Blue, I Love You Blue!

IV. I Am Waiting For My Train To Come In.

For Sandy,
my life's partner,
without whom
this book would not be possible

I

Sing aloud for the coming of the light!

THE GIFT OF SILENCE

> *God withdrew Itself*
> *from Itself into Itself.*
> —from the Kabbalah of
> Isaac Luria, 16th century Safed

In the beginning there is silence,
Then the sound of silence,
Then the sound.
Words pour forth out of our yearning
To name names:
        This is a tree, this a cloud,
        This an orange, this a blade of grass—
As if by naming them
We call them out of No-thing
Into Yes! Thing!
        This is a fish, this a bird,
        This bread, this wine.
A man comes forth,
        And we call him *Adam*—
        Earth Man.
A woman comes forth,
        And we call her *Chavah*—
        Life Force.

In the beginning there is silence,
Then the sound of silence,
Then the sound.
Words pour forth out of our yearning
To name the Nameless,
To touch with the yearning
In our voices
The Voiceless One
Who spoke
And the world came to be.

June, 1996

ONE-WAY WINDOW

Kol habasar chatsir . . .
All flesh is grass . . .
Isaiah 40.6

Cracks are widening on the silver surface
Of the one-way window keeping watch on my soul.
Now the light pours through in both directions,
Exposing thoughts and feelings on either side
Once nebulous and hidden from my view.

I ring the bell, but there is no one, no One
To answer my unarticulated plea,
To tame the silent demon crouching at the door
Urging me, urging me to reach, to reach for more,
For more—whatever, whatever that might be.
You, demon daring me, angel pushing me to a higher rung
Beyond extinction of all that I have ever done.

The window's cracking surface is a spider web of two-way truth.
I ring the bell again and again; *let me in, let me in!*
But there is no ear to hear, no eye to see,
No soft hand to soothe my still too fleshy me.

The foolish, frightful emptiness of waiting for Godot
To take me in Her holy arms, to comfort me,
To reaffirm the freeing fact that all flesh is grass—
The cruel, uncertain solace of damaged window,
                    scratched up glass.

July, 2010

SAND SPIRIT

> *Ehyeh Asher Ehyeh . . .*
> *I will be where*
> *I will be . . .*
> *Exodus 3.14*

You send sand swirling
Down desert dunes of empty beach,
Leaving Your signature of death
Upon shells of scallops, mussels, oysters, clams
Pounded into shards by winter heavy waves;
Scattered bones of driftwood laced with ice
Abandoned to the cold light of the four-o'clock sun;
The overturned carapace of a horseshoe crab
Picked clean by shrieking gulls, mad with hunger.

You breathe new patterns of sand sculpture
Through the open window of my melancholy,
Forming fresh fictions as in an ancient desert,
Hinting at the green Exodus that yet must come
Because You promised me Passover.

March, 1998

THE CLOISTERS IN WINTER

Glassed in for the season
Solemn still, stately, columned, cool
Dimly lit, a world of shadows
The January sun distant and cold

From the eaves icicles drip, drip dripping
In sympathetic syncopation with Gregorian chant
Sacred breath of melody, rising and falling
Rising and falling, the slow pulse of eternity
Piped in from Another Place, beckoning
Calling us with a gentle insistence,
As insistent as the pull of the tide,
Calling us to the impossible world
Of our broken dreams.

August, 2007

WHEN THE MORNING STARS SANG TOGETHER
(Job 38.7)

Sing aloud for the coming of the light!
Clap your hands for the dawning of the day!
Shout for joy at the passing of the night!

Choirs of crows, your death black wings bright
In morning sun, cackle, caw, pray:
Sing aloud for the coming of the light!

Soaring gulls in screeching sun-scorched flight
Above the flickering fish-filled spring tide bay
Shout for joy at the passing of the night!

My soul — it roars, it crackles, calls. My sight
Finds peacock feathers now. No more street-slush gray.
Sing aloud for the coming of the light!

My January burdens fly, now light
As air in sun-slant rays of greening May.
Shout for joy at the passing of the night!

Free! Free! Released from death-fear blight,
I celebrate myself, my God. I say:
Sing aloud for the coming of the light!
Shout for joy at the passing of the night!

May, 1996

MODEH ANI LIFANECHA

Modeh ani lifanecha, I give thanks to You
Who wakes me into soft morning light
Who spreads out the tent of the sky
Who flames the day with sunflower faces

Who wakes me into soft morning light
As gulls scream their hunger in loud, soaring flight
Who flames the day with sunflower faces
Burning and yearning for the death of the night

As gulls scream their hunger in loud, soaring flight
Who spreads out the tent of the sky
Burning and yearning for the death of the night
Modeh ani lifanecha, I give thanks to You.

Summer, 2004

JOY

Leaps!

Across morning meadow
With her laughing, lusty eyes,
Jubilant joy, jumping and bounding,
Red dress flower bright,
Face glowing, ruddy and radiant.

French sing *joie*
Joy rings joyful,
Joy bursting in air.
A-yo-DEL-le in Swahili.

No matter how we happen to breathe,
Aphrodisiac is still a five-Joy word!!!!!
Shoeless feet dance on fresh spring grass,
Buzzing
Humming

June, 1996

OUT OF AFRICA

From land-locked Mali, West Africa,
He steps on stage, robes flowing like the music
Soon to pour out of him.

He sits down on small stool, fingers engaging
The twenty-one strings of lute/harp
Called *kora*—cow skin stretched across calabash—
To send sound soaring.

The thumb of his left hand plucks a rhythmic base,
While the index finger of the same hand
Plucks out a line of melody;

His right thumb and index finger improvise
An accompaniment, an intricate filigree
Upon ten strings of higher pitch.

Eyes closed, he sits Buddha-like,
Channeling the sacred score flowing,
Flowing from Another Place.

November, 2009

THE BUDDHA ON BENEFIT STREET

The Buddha on Benefit Street: lotus-like,
Cross-legged, seven feet from knee to folded knee,
Massive head nine feet above the ground
On which he rests, anchored, impassive, eyes closed

To bring to focus the world within, a mirror
To the world without . . . distraction, pain, and death.
Your skin is cut from the mystery forests of Japan:
Cryptomeria—a hint of sacred secrecy.

Now you sit solitary in a room of your own,
In a quiet dark corner on an upper floor.
I bring you no prayer, no incense, no chant,
But the gift of my self, my quiet reflection.

My breathing slows in the glow of your presence;
I leave you renewed . . . the rest is silence.

October, 2009

ON VIEWING HIERONYMUS BOSCH

Garden of earthly delights, crowded ripeness of life,
Sweep me into your Medieval mind.

Awaken me to the energy of your bold brush,
The fecundity, the fertility of your inner eye,
Burst me into your spring tide bloom of blood
And fruit and flower and bone.

August, 2000

HERE AND NOW

You are *here*
maintaining détente
between the voices
in your head.

Rae Armantrout, *Paragraph*

I am *here.*
I am *now.*
I am trying
To maintain détente
Between the voices
In my head—

All that yin and yang,
That din and clang—

Between Yevtushenko's
City of Yes and City of No,
My wire stretched taut
Between your marmalade sun
And my unwashed longings,
Between her dish of delights
And his heavenly hatreds—

All that din and clang,
That yin and yang—

Squeezed like an orange
Between the blackness of before
And the blackness of ever-after,
My pulp runneth over
Into the tumult of today.

July, 2010

AND CAIN ROSE UP

Vayakum Kahyin,
And Cain rose up
In his wrath of rejection
Far from the garden, after the fall
Spitting his fury
At the face of his Father.

Vayakum Kahyin,
And Cain rose up,
And Cain rose up against Abel,
Against his brother and rival,
Spitting the curse
Of his impossible past.

Vayakum Kahyin,
And Cain rose up
Cursing tomorrow
With pounding fist.

Cursed by tomorrow
Branded forever
With a scarlet C
Etched into his face
With the acid fingers
Of his merciless Father—
The voice of his brother's blood
Crying out to us from the ground
Now and forever.

Summer, 2006

ESAU

> *. . . thus did Esau despise his birthright.*
>
> *Genesis 25.34*

For a bowl of stew
For a fifty-cent bowl of stew
Esau sells out his God
For some red lentils
He tells his father to go to hell
Chewing up his birthright
Swallowing his past
In huge gulps
He serves the god of stomach
His only pain
Hunger for the here and now
Gratify me!
Sweat drips down the nape of his hairy neck
As he wipes his wet mouth
With the back of his hairy hand

February, 1969

GOD'S TOOL BOX

God is lying on His back under the world,
Always busy repairing, something's always falling apart.
I wanted to see all of Him, but I see
Only the soles of His shoes and I cry.
And this is His praise.
from Yehuda Amichai, "And This is Your Praise"

From a respectful distance we observe God
Lying on His back under the world,
Busy, busy at His work of Repair.
I've given them a Cadillac,
And they leave me this jalopy.
The rumble of His discontent shatters the cosmos.
A mouse roars.

Neither of us can see God's face;
He is absorbed in the task of rebuilding
The ruined chassis; revitalizing the tired engine,
Replacing all the plugs to spark it back to life
Will have to come later.

On the floor of God's garage,
Stained with grease and drying pools of motor oil,
Sits a red metal tool box,
Heavy with the weight of the past;
Its four drawers are empty,
For God has spread out its contents
Upon the sports pages of yesterday's newspaper:
Rubber mallets for body work, hammers,
All the necessary nuts and bolts,
Screw drivers of similar shapes but varying sizes,
Including at least seven with Phillips heads.

Into the works a monkey wrench, of course,
Along with box wrenches, open-end wrenches,
Socket wrenches, and a complete set of 36 Allen wrenches,
Each one in search of its proper fit.
Male and female, I created them.

Sighing long and deep, God turns to us at last.
The beads of sweat on His brow
Dance the radiance of eternal youth,
While acid etched wrinkles proclaim Ancient of Days.
His gray eyes wear the pain of worry and regret:
Oy vey iz Mir!
I cannot fix this by My Self.

My friend Yehuda smiles his sad smile;
I wipe away my tears of joy.
And this is Your praise!
V'he t'he-la-TEH-cha!

October, 2009

THE PIT

Deep in the pit,
Ooze seeping
Through time-worn shoes
Already damp from sweating feet.
A six-inch centipede
Creeps out of dark slime—
Each twitching leg a silence,
Unseen mouth quivering, expecting . . .
No grip on smooth mud walls
For trembling fingers.

Or is this pit
The deep dark down nest
Of an enemy within
Who continues to pursue me
On many legs?

If only I could hear the echo
Of Your cry of absence
Calling me, calling me,
The echoing cry of Your absence,
The echoing cry . . .

                                        Autumn, 1996

UNCLE AMOS

Hear this word,
You cows of Bashan!
Amos 4.1

Is always shooting off his mouth
To the wrong people in the wrong places.
I mean, what can you do with bachelor of 35
Who storms into Bonwits on a Saturday afternoon
In loin cloth and sandals
And proclaims in basso profundo
All sales are final?

Oh, you cows of Scarsdale,
You who moo at his nearly naked self,
Your purple hair tells of youth lost at Avenue A,
Your wrists tinkle trivialities of fine gold.
Do you not know that Uncle Amos
Is a Chippendale dancer
On Sunday evenings
From 9:00 P.M.
Till closing?

January, 1990

GLASSES

At the very back of the dictionary
In the section marked BIOGRAPHICAL NAMES
I discover that Rasputin was a Russian mystic;
I have also learned he was an evil advisor to the tsar.
If he were a mystic, he might have journeyed
To within an eyelash of God—
The boundary between God and us
Being a narrow ridge that cannot be crossed.

I take my glasses off, I put them on.
The azalea blossoms and promises to blossom.
God is neither the object nor the subject.

God is the glasses the world wears to see
The evil advisor and the mystic dancing the hora
At the great wedding feast at the end of time.

                              Autumn, 1996

AT SEVENTEEN

At seventeen
Joseph tries on his coat of many colors
And begins to wear the garment
Of dreams which come true
And do not come true.

At seventeen
I try on the men
I become and do not become:
Ahab, raging at the dumb white whale:
In the midst of the personified impersonal,
         a personality stands here!
Dimitri Karamazov, diving headfirst
Into the bowels of degradation—
But even in the gutter
Refusing to renounce his Madonna.
King Lear, majestic in madness.

Today I park my wagon
         on a driveway paved with asphalt.
(The clam shells used to crunch under the weight
         of the 6:00 A.M. milk truck. A neighbor complained.)

My daughter no longer wears braces.

                         January, 1988

PURIM

If I were a dove,
I'd soar above the masks
Of blown-apart children,
Their blood drowning the stones
Of the Tel Aviv square;
And I would coo *shalom, salaam,*
As parents shake their fists at heaven
And at my blasphemy.

If I were a fish,
I'd swim to the depths
Of the great Salt Sea
To rescue the one living tear
Which could wash away forever
The ancient curse of Haman,
That millennial stain
On our millennial story.

The tear is both the salt of sorrow
And the water of laughter
Which turns death upside down
In a competition of tumblers
Under the big tent of the Messiah.

                              Spring, 2000

JOB'S ANSWER TO GOD

> *Then the Lord answered Job out*
> *of the whirlwind . . . Where were*
> *You when I laid the foundation*
> *of the earth?*
> *Job. 38.1,4*

So You think You've won
Just because You call me names—
Worm, cur, ant—
By implication, of course.

I admit it.
I wasn't there for the big event,
The one You got such a big bang out of
(Dangling preposition and all).
I haven't formed any galaxies lately
Or fashioned a planet
Or transformed even one green caterpillar
Into a blazing butterfly.
I can't even get my tie
To match my shirt.

You've made it clear that You are the ONE,
That MGM and Paramount cannot match
Your satin sunrises and velvet sunsets,
That we may call seas Atlantic and Pacific,
But it is You who keeps them filled.

Before I go, one last question:
Where were You
When I laid the foundation
Of my helplessness?

Winter, 1990

YOU!

> *. . . and a man wrestled with him*
> *until the break of dawn.*
> *Genesis 32.25*

You elude me like a name heard once.
You taunt me with demands I cannot meet
And cannot fail to meet.
Shall I strip off my anger like a bathing suit
      coarse with sand?
Shall I swallow my lust like a vitamin?
You call me to a yesterday I cannot face
And to a tomorrow far deeper than the river
      I have crossed.
Your sweaty arms drip insolence.
Your bony legs squeeze me to truth.

You! You! You!

August, 1996

BEFORE THE SILVER CORD IS SNAPPED
—Kohelet 12.6

Boy little not blue
Casts a sharp shadow
On green summer grass:
Something new under the sun.

His eyes drink delight
At lady bug beetle
On tanned boyish wrist,
A mere playful speck
Of purple-dot orange
On blond sun-bleached hair.

At the next breath of breeze
Ladybug beetle without much adieu
Joins dragonfly friends
In hot July air.

But winter will come,
A night of black ice.
The silver cord will be snapped
And the golden bowl shattered
For boy little not blue
      and ladybug beetle
           and dragonfly too.

                1990

BITTUL HAYESH:

EXTINGUSHING WHAT IS

*There is no room for God in
those who are full of themselves.*

*attributed to Baal Shem Tov,
1700-1760*

Climbing Jacob's Ladder
To beckoning void
At each rung I leave behind
Another garment of my self
     One red lust
          One violet envy
               A pair of green longings

Emptied
Naked
Shivering
Looking down
     My world
          Spinning
               Away

Summer, 1988

SOUNDS OF OUR PEOPLE

Oh, to be in love
With the sounds of our people:
Shofar blast, wild and harsh
Like the desert wind,
Unheard in the world at large,
Piercing our sleeping hearts.

Sound of Hebrew, soul-tongue
Of Abraham and Moses and Isaiah.
Voice of Israel today—word of poet,
Word of shopkeeper at the gate.

Sound of Yiddish—language of fiddler,
Garment workers' angry cry.

Soft Ladino sound of Sephardic minstrels,
Echo of exile.

Sound of God in the breath of the Psalmist
From the silence of before
Into the silence of ever after.

January, 2007

AND NOT ALL APPLES ARE RED

And not all apples are red,
And not all jealously is green.

A prism explodes the light beam's unity
Into the thousand colors of October—
Beyond the limits of violet,
Below the threshold of red.
Truth bends and breaks;
But is truth the prism,
Or is truth the beam of light?

Back in the Garden, she hands me the apple:
The snake told me to do it.
The apple is red as blood, and I take a bite.
Almost blinded by the furious disappointment
In God's green eyes, I turn away in shame,
The shame of now and forever.

October, 2009

THIS SMALL PIECE OF JERUSALEM

> *Jerusalem stone is the only stone that feels pain.*
> *There is in it a web of nerves.*
> *Yehuda Amichai, Jerusalem 1967, section 12*

This small piece of Jerusalem,
This Jerusalem stone, this *ehven Yerushalami*
Which sits so snugly in the palm of my right hand,
Takes me back to that still warm November evening
When I stood alongside my teenage David
On the nearly deserted Haas Promenade
Breathing in the sunset panorama to the north:
Golden walls of the Old City, graves in shadow
On the Mount of Olives, the "Y's" soaring spire
Holding hope for new beginnings in an ancient land.
Turning to my son in the fading light, I tell him:
Here we have lived for a hundred generations.
Reaching beneath a low green shrub, I pick up a stone
And place it my red knapsack.

Following night, Saturday night, on Israeli TV:
Crocodile Dundee with Hebrew subtitles
Until the rude interruption of block letters
Marching across the top of the screen . . .
HADASHOT HASHUVOT . . . HADASHOT HASHUVOT . . .
Next swirling moment fragmentary voices of frantic reporters . . .
SHALOSH YERIOT . . . RABIN B'VET HOLIM . . .
          MATSAVO KASHEH
IMPORTANT NEWS . . . IMPORTANT NEWS . . . THREE SHOTS . . .
RABIN IS IN THE HOSPITAL . . . HIS CONDITION GRAVE . . .

At Rabin's funeral his granddaughter's simple Hebrew words
Sing the song of her shattered innocence:
Forgive me for not speaking about peace.
I want to speak about my grandfather.

This small piece of Jerusalem,
This Jerusalem stone, this *ehven Yerushalami*
Which sits so snugly in the palm of my right hand,
Takes me forward to the darkness of my own casket,
Where I will sleep with this stone
The sleep of generations.

November, 2009

PATTERNS OF CIVILIZATION

A coil and a half of wisteria vine
Once wrapped around a backyard tree
Four full feet if stretched straight
Copper colored, brown blotched
Now screwed into a driftwood base
One end sanded to a smooth and graceful tail
One end shaped to suggest a serpent's head
Two turquoise beads become a pair of unseeing eyes
The mouth—a simple slit from which protrudes
A lifeless forked metal tongue
Never to dart fiercely
This way or that

A stone of irregular shape
It covers the palm of my hand
And fills my fingers
As I gauge its weight
Its color attracts:
Pinkish brown patched with white
This stone turns gold
In the slanting rays of the rising and setting sun
This stone feels pain, the poet tells us
There is in it a web of nerves.
Jerusalem stone

The pipe is virgin briar
A streaky reddish brown
A miniature tenor sax
Without the shining valves
The bowl has not tasted tobacco
Or music for twenty years

Three objects in imperfect dialogue
Patterns of civilization
Shades of brown
A tamed briar, a half-tamed vine
And a stone untamed as the ancient hillside
From kingdom come

                    Autumn, 1996

THE SOUND OF THE LETTER S

Hissing asp slithering scaly-skinned
Across sun-soaked stone.
Call me Snake, call me *Schlange,*
Call me *Nachash*, sly serpent
Ending Eden.

SS: Black-shirted *SchutzStaffel,*
Apostles of pain, deliverers of death,
Their cold collars scarred by
Runic zig-zag insignia, the mark of Satan
Bleeding into sadistic smiles,
Conscience under siege
By an all-consuming senselessness.

Hear the hell hiss of Zyklon B
Ssssss into hope-choked chambers.
Nothing left
But the anguished rasp
Of last gasps.

May, 2008

THE NOW OF GOD'S EYES SMILING

> *A man and a woman*
> *Are one.*
> *A man and a woman and a blackbird*
> *Are one.*
> *Wallace Stevens, "Thirteen Ways*
> *of Looking at a Blackbird" (IV)*

I

A man and a woman
Are one.
A man a woman and the eyes of God
Are one.

II

God's eyes do not match
The color of blue shadow
On January snow.

III

They radiate greater warmth
Than you and I can know
But less heat than the fires of hell.

IV

I turn away from the pain
In God's gray eyes.

V

Her lavender eyes
Swim more passion
Than the ocean in August.

VI

His black eyes
Bind us in a sacred circle.

VII

God wears
Neither eye shadow
Nor mascara.

VIII

Her copious tears run rain drops
Down His anguished face.

IX

The eyes of God shine rainbows
Through the mist of Her tears.

X

When God closes Her eyes,
The Milky Way darkens
Into the sadness of infinity.

XI

The fearsome gaze of God's eyes shoots
Poison arrows through the hearts of His enemies.

XII

I do not know which to prefer:
The now of God's eyes smiling
Or just after.

XIII

We are the eyes of God.

February, 2008

MOTHER OF LIFE

Mother of life
Breast milk flowing ever fresh and free
You birth and rebirth our pulsing, blood bloom world
Newborn's cry, death's final rattle, spring rain's renewal
Young grass pushing through hard April earth
Your energy is ecstasy
You set the stars dancing in whirling constellations
Your breath vibrates reeds and strings to sing new songs

Unto *Yah!*

Autumn, 1996

II

The white cliffs beckon still.

෨ ෨

FIRST MEMORY

My first memory is not about an apple
Or a green and brown snake or a booming voice
Asking me how I found out that I am naked.

Truth be told, I do not know how old I am
When I step off the gray curb
At the crosswalk. The light is green.
My little hand is in her big hand,
A hand which feels so strong to my weak hand,
A woman who seems so tall to my short legs
There in the gray shadow of gray buildings,
Small New Jersey city, Elizabeth, 1940's.
The hand of my mother.

Years pass and, truth be told,
The woman has shrunk, her hand has weakened.
In the morning I call her mother still.
By noon I am her father,
Which is not altogether untrue;
Nor is it true that I am not
In the garden after all, eating that apple,
Trying to hide from that booming voice
Asking how I found out that I am naked.

August, 1992

MY MOTHER'S WORDS

My mother never could keep her words straight;
They were always tumbling out of her mouth,
Pebbles spilling off a cliff.

She would whir through the kitchen
Like a bat out of water
In search of a jar of blackberry jam
Lost in a refrigerator deeper than Yonkers.
Voice soft as ice cream in August,
Mother would mutter to her lip-licking children:
It just went in one eye
And out the other!

Summer, 1994

I NEVER TOLD ANYBODY

I never told anybody that my Aunt Ann
Never was Cleopatra. No, never.

Or that I was afraid to set foot in a barber shop
Until my mother would say those magic words:
No shave! No shave!

I never told anybody that Phyllis Goldberg
Used to annoy me with her baby talk
About the '*ittle*' boy next door.
Don't say 'ittle,' I insisted, *say 'wittle.'*

You've got to believe me:
My Aunt Ann never was Cleopatra!

I never told anybody that I have never grown up,
That I am still in the back seat of a yellow Chevy,
Not watching the double feature I don't remember,
Entwined forever in the arms of
I never told anybody.

August, 1996

BRONX KITCHEN

I don't remember where the oven was
Or the sink
What I do remember is this:
A crazy dumbwaiter that ate garbage
Be careful, Jimmy, you don't fall in.

The window opening to a courtyard
Dark and sooty, deprived of light
Clotheslines dripping with all kinds
Of non-kitchen embarrassments
Bras and panties and dead socks
Making their exits and their entrances
Through that lone window

A table for two if you were little
For only one if you were grown
Large enough to hold one bowl of grandma's soup
Barley and vegetables that smelled of Lithuania

She smiled at my five-year old face
Spoke to me love words in a language
I could not comprehend
Went back to her newspaper
Whose alphabet I did not yet know
Grandma Ida's kitchen

Until Aunt Ann dashed in
With her flaming red hair
And brassy Bronx voice

Summer, 1995

THE LIZARD OF '47

I am there too,
All three years old of me,
Linden, New Jersey, the night after Christmas,
When God in the shape of my father
Bursts through the front door,
Stamps his boots to shake off the snow,
Throws off his snow-crusted overcoat
And informs the three of us
In his bear of a voice:
THERE'S A LIZARD OUTSIDE!
My mother and my seven-year-old sister
Seem unconcerned, as does my brother;
For he won't be born for another two years.
But I am quaking; I can see
In the eye of my little boy's mind
This giant green lizard—
The kind that later will appear
In the Japanese horror movies of the 1950's—
Stalking across our front lawn,
Leaving deep prints of its webbed feet
In the gathering snow,
Its red beady eyes searching for a way
To breach the security of our castle.

It is a couple of days
Before we can dig out our driveway.
Somehow I mange to lose my left boot,
Which will stay buried
In a mountain of shoveled snow
Until the melt of March.

July, 2001

FIREFLIES

Memories of summers past
When I could still walk barefoot
On the evening grass,
Washed out jelly jar in hand,
Chasing flickering lights,
Intimations of my own mortality,
Though I could not know that then,
Decades before my body started
Collapsing upon itself,
Not quite crushed by the double weight
Of years and experience—
August innocence ever so slowly
Traded in for January wisdom.

Three lights start to dim
In the washed out jelly jar.
Time to come in! Time to come in!
With a twist of my right hand,
             I open the jar.

Three fireflies escape into the night sky.

                       Summer, 2006

DREAM RIDING

riding and riding and driving and driving
bicycle bicycle car car
I come to a crossroads
rain-slicked and cool

bicycle bicycle car car
voices within voices without
rain-slicked and cool
I don't want to I want to

voices within voices without
mad journal tells all
I don't want to I want to
no I don't yes I do

mad journal tells all
spaghetti street tangles lead away and away
no I don't yes I do
no exit no entrance no time for fair play

spaghetti street tangles lead away and away
fantasies rages after the fall
no exit no entrance no time for fair play
Kerouac-kept secrets answer the call

fantasies rages after the fall
where is that crossroads
Kerouac-kept secrets answer the call
riding and riding and driving and driving

October, 2008

THE EDGE OF THE BRONX

And after assorted bed springs and treadless tires
And one or two foodless refrigerators,
We discover a trestle
Which spans with two steel rails and occasional planks
A river called the Bronx.
Because it is a trestle,
Because it goes someplace,
And because it is May,
We cross above the rowboats
To a keep-out world of live third rails,
High voltage, barbed wire.

Escaping at last,
We feel the river grass tickle our ankles.
Slender giraffe necks of adolescent trees
And tall pink apartment houses
Poke at the white, fair weather clouds.
One brown boulder interrupts the flatness
Of the green field spread out before us.
In the distance, Long Island Sound, a strip of blue
Dotted with white sails puffed by the four o'clock breeze.
To our left and far away, the regal span
        of the Throg's Neck Bridge
Shines silver in the light of spring.
Breathing in the cool excitement of flowing grass and water,
We stroll into the freshness of late afternoon.

Spring, 1963

ETTA! ETTA!

JULY 4, 1962

I.

Etta! Etta is your name.
You live in Iowa.
I didn't know that Jews live there now.
Born when I was born, 1940's
Your hair is black, your body ripe,
Lips moist, tongue eager
To explore the inside of my mouth,
No fear of falling.
One hour of innocence in a white life boat,

Snuggling, sheltered
     by a tarp from the North Atlantic wind.
The crew are Italian. They stand in shadows,
     protect us,
Avert their eyes in silent, loving complicity.
See the moon dance broken beams
An ocean away from Ambrose Light,
     Ms Aurelia.

Do you remember the high noon sea
Celebrating her own independence,
Patchwork quilt of green and blue
     and foaming white,
Waves parading under white cloud
     strong sun blue true sky?

Tomorrow the white cliffs of England.

II.

That was then.
Before the golden bowl was shattered,
Before JFK was shot dead
One loveless Friday afternoon,
Bus fumes in Port Authority
        choking our sorrow,
Before the news of King's assassination
Splintered the spring evening
        of our young marriage—
Sandy and I, Inwood apartment,
        kitchen view of a brick wall.
Before our daughter began to smile,
Before our son saw the light of day,
Before mother's descent
        into the maelstrom of madness,
Before all those births
        and deaths and rebirths . . .

III.

Before you, Diane,
      jumped off the Golden Gate.
Were you too proud to call me
Out of the abyss of your fatal grief?
Look! Here is the snapshot you sent me.
      Coney Island.
Your toothy grin, my crew cut,
      your flowing hair kissing my cheek.
         Your words, Diane,
Your delicate hand on a note card,
      April 8, 1971:
No matter how many times
      one reviews the past,
The present is still what it is.
And now you swim
      in the depths of am-no-more,
A fish, forever mute.
If only I could pull you out
      of your cold, salt bath.

IV.

Oh, Etta! Etta is your name.
Where are you now?
Some leafy street in suburban Des Moines?
Two station wagons, two kids in college,
     an aging collie?
A pot-bellied husband
     who drinks too much beer
And makes too much money
     for you to run free?
Are you out on your own,
     alone in your studio,
Painting your bitterness
     on small canvasses that sell
Rather well in fixed-up brick-wall galleries
On gentrified, hazelnut downtown streets?

V.

Talk to me, Etta! Remember me!
Come with me back to the snug harbor
Of our white lifeboat out of the Atlantic wind
An ocean away from Ambrose Light.
I am here, Wednesday, July 4, 1962,
     almost midnight
         and today
            and tomorrow.

The white cliffs beckon still.

Spring, 1996

125 SEAMAN AVE.

There are no trees on Seaman Ave.,
North of the Cloisters, Manhattan.
Why would anybody want to live here?
My sister asks, her question shaped
By her large house in a leafy Jersey suburb.

The apartment is spare, a railroad flat.
Front door opens to a long hall;
At the far end, small bathroom:
Working toilet, shower, sink.
First left, a tiny kitchen,
Window facing a brick wall,
The stark set of Jackie Gleason's *Honeymooners*.
Second left, a living room/dining room;
The view is not much better.
Final left, the bedroom: adequate but no closet.
The view . . . . courtyard strewn with garbage.

The building is not wired for air conditioners.
In the summer, we distribute one bath towel
For each dinner guest. Nobody complains.
Late at night the roaches scramble
With the flick of the switch
Of the bathroom light.

First home, early marriage, 1968.
What can you expect
For a rent control rate of $79.66?

April, 2009

ALLEN'S LION

I came home and found a lion in my living room . . .
Allen Ginsberg, The Lion for Real, 1958

I come home and find a lion in my living room
Run to the phone, dial my wife, and pant,
Honey, there's a lion in our living room!

Why do these things always happen to us?
And the rug was just cleaned!
She hangs up.

In comes Mary in search of two fresh eggs
And one teaspoon's worth of vanilla extract.
Jim, do you realize there's a lion in your living room?
She walks out.

The phone rings; it's my father.
He's in his eighties but refuses to retire.
Dad, there's a lion in our living room!

I'm so proud of you, Jim.
Send me the picture when it appears in the paper.

With a swish of his shaggy mane,
The lion exits left,
Straight through the closed screen door,
Trampling the dandelions on the front lawn.

May, 1996

EVENING SONG

One winter evening the sleet
Bangs an angry song upon our gutters.

Backyard hydrangeas—
So hard to sense their subtle shades
In the evening in the lingering light.

Three skunks—black and white and fearless—
Visit our barbecue,
The air is filled with mosquitoes,
Ghosts fly freely among the bats.

Is it harder to hate in the evening?
Easier to love?

The two of us walk down to the sea
In the evening, but clouds obscure
The drama of the setting sun.

Summer evenings are forever in these parts;
December evenings are swallowed whole
By snowy afternoons—the long night
Turning off the light without and within.

I do not know which to prefer:
The darkening blue of an October evening
Or the brightening blue of a morning in June?

I am prepared to wait all evening
At the phone which will never ring
For the voice I shall never hear.

Summer, 2004

BOTTOM LINE MAN

My father was a bottom line man
Probably because he grew up poor—
Never quite sure when the next dollar would come
To support him, older brother, three older sisters.
It hurt that his mother never did speak English;
She came from the Old Country,
Where the language was Yiddish.

No stored-up yearning in my little boy eyes
Could persuade him to cosset my head
On his unyielding lap. That was mother's job
Out in the suburbs during those postwar years
When "the buck stops here."

As a child he played on hard city streets;
Yet he heard ripe nature strumming alternate beats.
He could turn a few slivers of sassafras bark
Into the magic of sassafras tea.
He could read the maples by the shape of their leaves—
Norway, sugar, silver, Japanese—
And could tell the difference between a pine and a spruce.
He thrilled to the catkins drooping down from the willows,
To the lilac charged air of Spring letting loose.

August, 2010

SINCE BEFORE I CAN REMEMBER

Since before I can remember
I have been flying in and out of my dreams
Swimming through the air Australian style
Pushing and pulling my arms
Fluttering my legs two yards above
The flowing carpet of the waterless living room

A sharp right into the kitchen
Around the butcher block table
Then straight towards
The white refrigerator door
Not once making contact
With the scratched vinyl tiles
Which pattern the floor

Now I peddle the bicycle
Which is not there in the air
Spinning those wheels
Keeps me six feet above
The newly mowed lawn
Beating the alternative
Of six feet under

Summer, 2001

NIGHTMARE

My pulpit perch is three stories
Above the congregation.
They look up to me. I look down at them.
One step to the right, one step to the left,
And I tumble into the void.
My legs are putty, stomach in my feet.
I do not belong here.

I speak loudly, almost a scream
To make myself heard by the crowd below:
Please turn to page . . .
The pages are out of order.
Page 83 . . . page 16 . . . page 29 . . .
They fly out of my binder
And float down into the void
Like paper gliders.

Why doesn't he begin?
What is he waiting for?
He's been futzing around up there
For fifteen minutes . . .

Unable (or unwilling) to see the pleading in my eyes
Or to hear the pounding of my heart,
They pick themselves up ever so slowly
And, one by one,
Exit left.

Summer, 1995

ABOVE THE GULLS' URGENT CRIES

Today above the gulls' urgent cries,
The icy tail of jet plane five miles high,
White ribbon straight as the arrow of time—
That line which defines what is yet to be
In the deep sky sea of eternity.

From where I stand at the river's salt edge,
Eyes forced to squint in the fierce winter light,
The plane seems to streak east, Jet Stream propelled
Along with the baggage of her passengers' dreams—
Gaudi's melting houses on Barcelona streets,
Prague's Charles Bridge sculptures caught by the sun,
Bursting bright Paris in the dark of the year
Dream on, you skybirds, you have nothing to fear.

As the plane disappears, white tail in retreat,
The gulls shriek and dive, cold clams in their claws—
They drop them like bombs on the hard rock below
Then glide down for their meat, a taste of the sea,
Which they pick bit by bit from the crush of the shells.

November, 2007

SHADOW

My shadow trails along the winter sidewalk;
My hat of Russian fur hangs earflaps against the cold:
Right boot, left boot, proud and purposeful
I stretch my stride so as not to be late.

In a brown paper bag a pocket burst of vegetables
And a Granny Smith,
The meeting being meat-free.

my shadow sees
what I do not see
the dance of daylight upon the snow
the chandeliers of ice
the living shapes of frozen breath
pouring out of the mouths of passers-by
like balloon conversations in comic strips

Summer, 1999

LENINGRAD IN '88

The apartment blocks—massive, faceless—
Hide their entrances and their exits:
Visitors not welcome.

Quintessence of caution:
Don't speak to strangers.
Don't speak.
Don't.

Go only to the bank to change dollars to rubles.
The man in the shadows offers more
Without scruples and without fail
Will see you dragged off to a Soviet jail.

We dare not meander through the snowdust streets,
No muttering retreats. The police or KBG
Stop all who linger or malinger.
An ever so slight glimmer of light
Peeking under an undistinguished door
Calls us from the cold November night
Into a furnace-hot cellar, the color of coal,
Up, up a shoddy lift
To deliver the goods,
To accomplish our goal.

An infusion of vodka,
I look down at my shoes:
My socks do not match.
I am chilled through and through.

                                    August, 2010

BIRDSONG

Explosion of sound in our chimney
Desperate beating of wings
Against brick walls

Three quick steps to the flue
Open it . . .

Out she comes
Whirlwind of feathers

Large crow darker than soot
Knocks over two porcelain lamps
And thirteen onyx chess pieces

Crow's feet play frantic John Cage
On the keys of our untuned piano

                              July, 1997

EIGHT WEEKS AND COUNTING

Angel in my arms
Eyes softly shut
In dreamless sleep
Body curled, almost a ball
As if back in the womb.
You're a snake charmer,
Her father tells me.

But then angel face
Puts on the petulant scowl
Of a great-grandfather
She will never know—
The man who could spot the one nick
In a perfect bedroom bureau—
Her scowl twisting into urgent rage:
Feed me! I'm hungry!

Mother's breast milk feeds
A smile of contentment,
A return to angel face
Which lasts and lasts and lasts

Until the howl of her mouth shatters
That polished bronze visage
Framing an ancient echo of a scream
Which reverberates so shrilly
Among the newly painted walls
At MoMA.

Summer, 2007

HOMAGE TO ARCHIBALD MACLEISH

A poem should not mean
But be—"Ars Poetica"

You told me that forty-five years ago,
And you were right.
Although at the time, in my teenage inexperience,
When I knew that I would live forever,
When I had no need for some artifice of eternity,
Some Yeatsian Byzantium to shield me from the onset of nothingness,
I could not know why you where right
Or how you were right,
Only that you were right.

Senior year in high school:
Just before the big launch into the Big World,
Which for me turned out to be
The Big Apple just across the Hudson,
Our class was engaged in dubious battle
With *The Brothers Karamazov.*
For me, an opportunity to try on the men
I was to become and not become:
Ivan—the intellectual, piercing but sterile;
Dimitri—the sensualist, undisciplined, wild,
Who even in the gutter of degredation
Refuses to renounce his Madonna;
And then, and then Alyosha,
Who in the final pages sums it up:
Love life more than the meaning of it!

Over the mixed metaphors of the ensuing years,
It is Alyosha whose voice has called me, called me:
And so it is that I have chosen
Not to make my poems mean
But to let them be.

April, 2008

MY DAUGHTER'S REFRIGERATOR

My daughter's refrigerator contains
More on the outside than within
A controversy of magnetic moments

Plastic letters of the alphabet in primary colors
Spread out at random across the door
Waiting for some master poet
To fashion them into a primal scream
Of joyful babies, babies all around,
Babies smiling bright-eyed Season's Greetings
Babies loving laughter, babies laughing love
While one intense toddler presses his cheek
To the swell of momma's pregnant belly

And my granddaughter's finger paintings
Drip promises of a future
Pink and silver and aquamarine

Off to one side hang Yitzhak Rabin's blue on white words:
Ahdifah derekh ha-shalom meyasher derekh ha-milchamah
I prefer the way of peace to the way of war

My daughter's refrigerator
Contains more on the outside
Than within.

April, 2008

FRAGMENTS OF A NEW ENGLAND SUMMER

It is inconceivable in July
To call our world incomplete.
The June bugs have finally crawled out of their darkness
Into the soft light of the summer moon.
The moist melding of earth and sky
Breeds a fecundity of frogs croaking, bats skittering,
Crickets rubbing their hind legs in the heat of the night,
Chirping, chirping, chirping July delight.

Such a splash!
Three-pound bass misses a frog supper
On the glassy surface of a lake in Maine.

Gut'm! My father orders.
The sun plays hide and seek among the white summer clouds,
Casting shadows of blue and green over the scene.
A stray ray dances upon the bloody mass,
A study in scarlet. *They're eating crayfish,*
I tell him. I take from the burst stomach
The half-eaten critter, only one claw remaining.
Smell of pine sweetens the smell of death.

A bare-branched dying elm
Fades into an eerie silhouette
Back-lit by the afterglow of the August sun.

Sunflowers throw their smiles
Towards the blue of a new day:
Proud protoplasm,
Without guilt or nostalgia,
Erect
Until first frost.

August, 2008

THE TREES THEY DO GROW HIGH

The trees they do grow high
On either side of the leaf-strewn path
Leading to a sliver of blue sky
Where the sun never sets
At the far side
Of the man
I am
Forever
Becoming.

August, 2010

THE SHAPE OF MY WIFE

The shape of my wife
Is not at all the shape
Of a Bosc pear,
For which I am grateful.
She is not big at the bottom
And slender on top.
Her lines extend
Where they ought to extend
And contract
Where they ought to contract
Not quite an hourglass,
But even Eve
Could do no better
At 53.

May, 1996

BITTER LEMON

Neither round nor oval, humble in shape,
Imperfect as the world from which you sprang—
Were you with Adam? With Eve? The haunted snake?
On which dark tree of Eden did you hang?

Sunny compliment to our cup of tea—
Here we sit, face to face, heart to false heart,
Warmed by the illusion we are free
While drowning in each other from the start.

The smile of your skin masks the pain inside—
A bitterness that sets all teeth on edge
As hope and hope continue to collide
And bring to ashes every youthful pledge.

For all in the end cannot be harvest;
Persistence of memory mocks our rest.

August, 2005

RAPTURE AT 6:00 A.M.

Morning light of high summer
Spilling through wide windows facing south and east,
Transforming the breakfast nook into a blaze of possibility.
Breeze—still cool from the sunless night—
Breathing through the screens.
No sound but the refrigerator's subliminal hum.

In my glass breakfast bowl
A hill of voluptuous strawberries from California,
Heavy with the repressed promise of the taste to come.

Now paint the red fruit with the cool white of vanilla yogurt,
Add the unrepentant green extravagance
Of mint chocolate chip,
And finish with a blush of orange marmalade
Upon the toasted halves of an English muffin well done.

July, 2010

MASS PIKE COFFEE:

May 19, 2008, 1:30 P.M.

Lav Azza
Italy's favorite
Dark brown brew
Moist nurturing loam
Breath of espresso
Breath of Rome
City of steps
Leading from past to future
From future to past

Here I sit
Sipping, savoring
The forever of now
The remembrance of tomorrow

III

Blue, blue, I love you blue!

  ✑   ✑

BLUE!

Blue, blue, I love you, blue!

Blue your dreams seeking solutions
To wordless blue riddles.

Blue your thighs,
Blue your smile,
Blue the cool buzz
Of your sweet talk.

Blue the untamed energy
Flowing free
Through the wilds of your blue hair
From the heights of your depths
To the depths of your heights
Before the fall and after the fall

Until the blue blanket of peace
Spreads over us

Until
The blue kingdom
Comes.

Summer, 1998

HOWL AGAIN

> *I saw the best minds*
> *of my generation . . .*
> *starving hysterical naked . . .*
> *Allen Ginsberg, Howl, 1956*

I see the best minds of my generation

Starving for the naked truth of a naked lunch,
Honest meat. Forget the processed cheese,
The rationalizations and bastardizations, the obfuscations,
The accumulating adulterations of the pure products of America,
The furious uncurious fanaticism, the dance of spin and folly—

Driven to hysteria by the madness of misused and much abused words,
The poisonous manipulation of jaded high-paid debasers
Who continue to insist that War is Peace,
That Ignorance is Knowledge,
That Falsehood is Truth,
That Blasphemy is Holiness
And that Holiness is Blasphemy,
Who hold that torture is not torture,
Who hide what is self-evident under the filthy veil
Of "extraordinary rendition" and "extreme physical pressure"—

Naked and alone among mass media marketers
Who drive our nation's lemmings
      into an unforgiving ocean of incomprehension,
Who pollute the minds of our children with dreams
      that can never come true,
Who sell new and improved video games
      featuring new and improved violence,
Who sell tight-fitting jeans in 10,000 styles,
Who sell 47 varieties of gourmet cat food,
Who sell 100 bottles of beer on the wall,
Who sell our souls to the highest bidder—
Devil or not, here we come!—

So that the starving and the hysterical, the best of our generation,
Have nothing better to do than to take off their clothes
And go to New Hampshire
To live free or die.

February, 2008

Notes: *Naked Lunch,* 1959, is an experimental novel by William Burroughs.
    "The pure products of America" is the opening line of a poem by William
    Carlos Williams, "To Elsie", 1923.
    See also Allen Ginsberg's "On Burroughs' Work", 1954, first collected in
    Reality Sandwiches.

THE DICE IS ROLLING

The dice is rolling out of the cup
Tumbling towards me through the air
As in a mind-twisting painting
By Salvador Dali
Drawing me against my will
Into the brush strokes of his overstuffed dreams

More melting watches, more crawling ants
Persisting in his memory as well as in mine
A tiger bursts forth from the mouth of a fish
A key to the tomb of our own buried fears

The buzz of a fly
'round a half-eaten pomegranate
The sound of this summer
Of our half-eaten year

August, 2003

AFTER THE RAIN

Response to
After the Rain, oil on canvas,
Anthony Tomaselli

After the rain
The sky is pale blue.
The returning sun splashes
A puddle of light upon the cobblestones.

A lone young man, hair black,
His short-sleeved red shirt
The color of the red-tiled roofs
Topping the time-worn buildings
Of terra cotta clay—
Color of earth, color of then—
The lone young man a living contradiction
To this empty street.

Behind him and to his left
An ancient archway,
Half-hidden, half-revealed
Like those entrances and exits
He has already passed through
And is yet to pass through.

He is riding an old bicycle,
A basket of bread on the handlebars.
Ahead of him, the gathering shadows;
Ahead of him, at least one home waiting for bread,
Delivery delayed by the onset of rain.

A quiet corner
In the abundance of Italy.
Abbondanza.

October, 2008

BALL REVISITED

I think it was John Berryman
Who read his poem that winter night
And I was so much older then
When I followed the boy who followed the ball

Who read his poem that winter night
Bouncing down down a cobblestone street
When I followed the boy who followed the ball
Picking up speed with each bounce

Bouncing down down a cobblestone street
At a reckless, whizzing, dizzying pace
Picking up speed with each bounce
Past banana stand and watermelon man

At a reckless, whizzing, dizzying pace
One final bounce and at last a big splash
Past banana stand and watermelon man
The ball buried itself in the harbor of doom

One final bounce and at last a big splash
The boy could be not more than five
The ball buried itself in the harbor of doom
His tears tore the skin off the pale August sky

The boy could be not more than five
And I was so much older then
His tears tore the skin off the pale August sky
I think it was John Berryman

Autumn, 1996

MEXICAN MADONNA

Diego Rivera, Mexico, 1938

Infant wrapped tightly to bosom,
Small head turned toward the future,
Strong, confident charcoal lines,
The skin of her bonnet a moon without feature.

The mother is in profile, sombrero
Shielding her from the midday sun.
A gold ring—or is it silver?—
Hangs on the lobe of her left ear;
Eyes, staring straight ahead,
Nose, somewhat flattened, mouth half-opened
As if to take a tired breath,
Chin stone strong, face fierce with battles
Fought, fighting, to be fought.

Though you slay me, yet will I endure!

Hardy peasant stock,
From generation to generation.

May, 1996

SEA SMOKE

Ten below zero. Rare for these parts.
The river ice flows south with the ebbing tide.
Out of the grey pockets of salt water, still ice free,
The sea smoke rises—young mothers in virgin white robes,
Hands held high to the brightening sky.

A faint breath of breeze, and the vapor freezes
To the bare limbs and the evergreen needles
On the Western shore.

Caught in the first rays of the rising sun,
Trees explode into a symphony of crystal.
Thundering silence of a January morning,
The still, small voice of a new day.

July, 2005

SHAWL

The shawl, I found out later,
Was made in China, pure silk;
But the shoulders it draped
In the cool of that evening
Belonged to a Latina.
I do not know her name or her age,
Only that the delicacy
Of the sheer and shimmering silk
Seemed to contradict the hardness
Of her strong and defiant body,
A body shaped by years in the fields
Bending and lifting, bending and lifting.

I saw her only once—
Twilight, at the well,
Like Rachel, drawing water.
As she turned away,
A bucket hanging heavy in each hand,
A puff of breeze lifted the shawl
From her brown-skinned shoulders
And blew it gently
Into the Mexican dust.

                              Summer, 1999

APPLE IN OCTOBER

Crisp surprise of New England autumn,
Wrapped in paper thin skin of red and green,
Tart as that clipped talk, that felt reticence
Which suggests that good fences make good neighbors.

This apple, here—in this fruit bowl, so very real,
Real as the lengthening shadows of our fall afternoons,
Real as the deepening darkness night after night,
Real as the shortening sunlight,
The increasing bitterness of the northeast wind
Bringing in its breath the smell of soon-to-fall snow.

Not some mythical fruit in some mythical garden,
But this apple, here—in this fruit bowl.

And now, apple in October,
So tempting and so tart,
The time for tasting you has come.

October, 2007

A MEAL WITH THE LADY NOT THERE

This really happened
In an open-air restaurant in Bermuda
On the top of a hill amidst hibiscus and palmetto
Just outside of Hamilton, at sunset,
Sometime during the last decade
                of the Twentieth Century:
He ate the entire meal by himself—
All five courses—
Along with the lady not there.

The waiter serves the appetizer:
Maybe it is smoked bluefish,
Maybe it isn't.
The man arranges and rearranges
The plates, the glasses, the napkins, the roses.
He focuses his camera and refocuses.
He takes a picture. Click.

The soup is possibly a seafood bisque.
He takes a picture.

Perhaps the salad holds endives.
A picture.

The main course should be filet mignon
With sauce Bernaise, wild rice,
And fresh asparagus.
Picture.

A whipped cream fruit torte.
Topped with four succulent strawberries,
Would make the perfect dessert.
Click.

The lady is in London.
The wine is red.

Summer, 1998

PRO CRAS

> *pro:*
> the Latin word for forward
> *cras:*
> the Latin word for tomorrow

Why ruin today
With what I can put off
Till tomorrow
Or tomorrow's tomorrow?
Let me fill my basket of today's desires
With yesterday's wishes
And by doing nothing
Prolong desire as dream
Unfulfilled, yet ripening and reddening
Like the apple in the garden
Before Adam and Eve spoiled it
By taking their first bites.

Summer, 2002

THE PROBLEM WITH THE POMEGRANATE

The problem, said mother,
With the pomegranate
Which Eve plucked
From that tree in Eden,
Devouring its sweet flesh
In blind enchantment
Before taking the plunge
Into the rhetoric of life,
Is its full red fury,
Its remorseless, deep,
Unforgiving stain.

Summer, 2006

AT THE KATIE BROWN MEMORIAL FOUNTAIN

Your life was our joy,
Your death our teacher.

Wooden bench, blood red clouds of August twilight.
Uncommon coolness for this time of year:
Feel of late September, a surprise of fall,
A fooling of the senses so that I can almost smell
The decay of October, almost hear
The crackle of dead leaves under hard leather shoes.

And that smell of decay, that sound of dead leaves under foot
Breeds a certain sadness, causing me to wonder, Katie,
If you are somehow still here, a nourishing presence,
A promise of new grass pushing through hard April earth
Watered by the tears of all those who love you.

August, 2007

ANARCHY OF OPPOSITION

The anarchy of August in these parts
Not at all like the anarchy of February
Dripping, slipping, sloshing, slushing
Skiddeth bus and *sloppeth* us
Parking lots piled high with ice and snow
Virginal whiteness long since soot sullied
Cigar butts, soda bottles, beer cans
Brown and yellow evidence of dogs and cats
No need to hold it in. *Lhude sing Goddamm.*

The anarchy of August too hot too sticky to bear
Noonday sun driving us madder than mad dogs
And Englishmen. Changing shirts hour by hour
Sweat oozing, dead thoughts snoozing
In the haze and the daze of primitive comfort need
To find shade, to cool off, to escape the blasted furnace
Melting us to confess that we never should have cursed
The anarchy of February. *Sing goddamm, DAMM.*

October, 2007

Words in *italics* from "Ancient Music" by Ezra Pound

THE FOUR SEASONS

North wind sculpts white drifts
Blue shadows kiss the icy air
January laughs

Hard April earth begins to yield
Clouds cry tears of greening rain
Leaves of grass sing a new song

Sunflowers throw their smiles towards the sky
Proud protoplasm, erect
Until the first frost

Kicking leftover leaves
Boots laced tight against the cold
Colder still to come

Summer, 2006

PERHAPS THE SHAPE OF A ROBIN

Your silhouette is a gray blur
In the freezing fog of early morning March.
You hold the shape of a robin returned home—
Or perhaps you do; I can't be sure.
You stand so solitary
Upon the icy crust of whatever snow's remaining
Before the melt of April,
That final melt into spring.

Not for you the sublime grace, the delicate curves
Of the egrets who are yet to come,
Who are forced to wait for summer's warmth and light.
You are in shape solid, sensible, sound—
In shape to endure the lingering cold;
You wear the shape of true North.

                    March, 2009

ODE TO WINTER

You come!
I feel you in the smell of late October leaves.
I hear you in the sound of November's wind
Blowing leaves under leather boots
Laced tight against the chill.
I see you in lace-thin ice on puddle and pond
Yielding still to the noonday sun.
I hear you in the soon-to-cease
Honking of southward flying geese.

Now you are here,
Wrapped in snow sheet blizzard blowing white,
Snow dunes shaped and reshaped by wolf-howl wind.
Pine trees throw blue shadows
Upon still drifts in four o'clock light.
Your nights hang silent with ice,
Your nights of frigid and terrible silence,
A silence to end all silences

Until spring comes.

                                    Autumn, 1996

CLIFF WALK

The sound of the tide licking
Smooth stones that silken evening
Under the diffuse glow of the August moon

Was like the sound of God breathing
Like no other sound in Rhode Island . . .

Summer, 1990

MAYA ANGELOU READ A POEM

Maya Angelou read a poem
Yesterday, not any day,
Inauguration Day
Her voice strong and clear and deep
Out of Arkansas, out of Africa,
Out of the angry hopeful soul of America.

The words Rock and River and Tree
Primary words
As primary as red and blue and yellow
Ring out from Capitol steps to chilled ears
Washington dream drunk in crisp January sun.

She sings our Amen rhythms
She stirs our President's blood
She is our trumpet.

God will not debit our account
For those hours we make music
For America.

January 21, 1993

I THE OCEAN

Tidal tug of longing
Great green fury
Raging to be free
Of shores which bind me
To man-made names:
Atlantic, Pacific . . . .

Mapless amoeba
I break my tears
Upon stone hearts.

Summer, 1990

PRODUCT OF INDIA

Reaching down into the bag of my dreams
Groping for that promised gift, unspecified
Not to be found. Sifting through my yesterdays
Searching for tomorrow, my fingers coming up empty.

Cool sand of moonlit beach
Indifferent grains falling through a narrow neck of glass
Following the iron law of gravity
Pointing towards the animal law of growth and decay:
From the moment of birth our future is shrinking
Into the fierce and menacing maw of time.

Look at me, you mortals, and despair!

Burlap bag, zippered, tamper proof
Four pounds of Basmati rice, 1.8 kilos
Naturally aromatic; in Hindi, *The Fragrant One*
Bombay original, product of India.

October, 2007

MY FECKLESS CHICKADEE

I met my feckless chickadee
At an oyster bar in Tennessee.

We both took lemon in our tea:
What a marvel of serendipity.

Though I loved her well, I could surely see
In her nitwit eyes that she hated me.

July, 2010

CITISCAPE

Three skyscrapers
Taller than giraffes
But not so lean or graceful
Take a drink from the cool
Pool of a passing cloud

A river flows through parallel walls
Mossy, mildewed windowless worlds
Throwing concrete shadows
Upon the jungle green deep

Seventy-two finless fish
Swim through a window
On the seventy-second floor
Looking for the ocean

While three dragonflies hover
Noiselessly above a rose garden
Awash in beer and an embarrassment
Of sausage and sauerkraut

August, 2000

LONE RANGER NO MORE

The Lone Ranger is getting married
Tomorrow night at 7:00 P.M.,
A simulcast by CNN
On line and on TV.

Tonto, no longer trusted friend,
No longer *Kemo Sabe,*
Runs a ragged used car lot
In deep downtown Canarsie.
Scout has been turned into carpenter's glue,
While Hi-Ho Silver is long since gray;
And beneath the mystery of that cold black mask
Lie two cheeks of light brown freckles,
Pug nose, an untrimmed blue mustache,
And a tattoo of Venus de Milo.

The Lone Ranger is getting married
Tomorrow night at 7:00 P.M.,
A simulcast by CNN
On line and on TV.

Now listen up, fans, and hear my call:
Bride goeth before a fall!

                              Summer, 2001

BLOOD ORANGE

Blood orange sun
Bleeds into the west
Shedding red robes
Upon cool rippled pond

Blood orange moon
Peels off the night's mask
And bleeds a soft beam
Upon lost lonely loon

Summer, 1998

COPULATION

Am, is be, are—copulatives all!
Doing what they need to do, naturally,
Without sweating or groaning
Or even breathing; they simply are
In their *isness*.
Conjunctions in the guise of verbs,
Connectives, unity words:

I *am* who I am.
Water *is* life.
To *be* is the living antithesis of not to be.
You and I *are*
Bits of stardust
Combined and recombined
Since the beginning of time.

Am, is, be, are—seed of all simile,
                sacred soil of metaphor.

                                    Summer, 1999

CREATURE

Carried with the current
Ebbing and flowing with the tide
Soft tentacles losing themselves in seaweed
Coloring the salt water purple

Swimmers fear me.
My beauty carries a sting.

I am not a man.
I abhor war.
I do not speak Portuguese.

Summer, 2006

MERMAID

Anima of the sea
Singer of salt
Keeper of wrecks and secrets
Silent storm beneath
The cool skin of moonbeam waves

Hair curling and spilling
Over ripe breasts
Undulating midriff flowing
Into a swim of fins and scales
Even Odysseus cannot resist
Your wordless call

Summer, 1999

PRIGGLE VERB INTRANSITIVE

priggle: *verb, intransitive, origin obscure*
To speak authoritatively out of both sides of ones mouth;
To make an obvious point with such imprecision
       that the educated listener (Hegelian or untainted)
       will be equally convinced of its truth and its untruth.
Synonym: to bloviate; Antonym: to tell it straight.

The Midwestern lexicographer, Simon B. Flatus,
Known in those parts for his terminal inventiveness,
Reports that the word first appeared in the past tense
On Wednesday, January 27, 1954, in Duluth, Minnesota,
Where the *North Woods Mirror* ran this headline under the fold:
PASTOR JOHANSON HOLDS CHURCH-GOERS CAPTIVE

. . . Johanson *priggled* for an hour or more
On the cosmic implications of three verses
From *the Gospel According to St. Matthew,*
Oblivious to the surprising severity of the morning's snow.
By the time he had finished, he and his flock were trapped
In the pale-blue clapboard church just outside of town
Until the plow came and freed them early Tuesday morning.
Apparently the 71 men, women, and children survived
Each other's company and the company of Pastor Walter
With the help of some Tater-Tot hot dish
Left over from the Saturday night social.
Most members of the church confess
They still have no idea of their Pastor's point.
No injuries were reported.

July, 2005

IT'S NOT ABOUT THE BANJO

response to a pastel
by Mary Cassatt,
The Banjo Lesson, 1893

It's not about the banjo,
Which shows neither strings nor frets
Nor a bridge on its drum,
A banjo which cannot be played,
Which can make no music.

The pastel strokes are quick, almost sloppy,
As if the artist is in a hurry
To get to the main lesson,
Which is not about the banjo at all

But about those two radiant faces,
Faces of mother and daughter,
Cheek to cheek,
Into which the artist pours
The sum of her wonder and delight.

The ruddy glow of the mother's cheeks,
Set off by raven black hair caught up in a bun;
The face of the daughter, a shade softer,
As if to suggest her still soft innocence.

Two sets of eyes focus upon the banjo
Which cannot be played, which can make no music
Except for the symphony of their enduring love.

December, 2007

MARGINAL WAY, OGUNQUIT

Crash, crash of incoming tide
Biting into rock hard edge of Maine
White spray dissolving into morning light
Stiff breeze backlash of yesterday's storm
Filling the sails of bobbing boats
Beyond the breakers

Ebb tide's slow release
Minute by minute exposing
Small patches of sand and pebble beach
At first barely perceptible
Then rapid unfolding of broad new space
Freed from the turbulent tug of cross currents
Freed from the whims of the Atlantic

Until the flood tide pays a return visit
To this same bare place
This same ever shifting boundary
Reshaping the competing domains
Of earth
Of sky
Of water.

September, 2008

ON LISTENING

TO ROY HARRIS' THIRD SYMPHONY

> *"He was in despair."*
> *"What about?"*
> *"Nothing."*
>
> *Ernest Hemingway,*
> *A Clean, Well-Lighted Place*

January hotel room, downtown Chicago, frost on the window
Four-o'clock sun almost set in the red sky
A single bed, scratched dresser, broken TV
One ugly lamp casting harsh light
Into dusty corners Cigarette ashes
The vacuum never found

Drumbeat strength of resignation
Nothing left to lose

Supper time. Shivering along icy streets
Towards a clean, well-lighted place
Where I shall dine alone

                                        June, 1996

HOMAGE TO WALLACE STEVENS

Shapely,
Like no other shape,
Its shadow an enigma.

Its color is the smell
Of late October leaves.
Its color is the sound
Of the November wind
Blowing leaves under leather boots
Laced tight against the chill.

It holds the light
Like nothing else.

May, 1996

SEA GLASS

homage to Wallace Stevens

A blue that's almost ice
I hold it to my eye
Translucent
Light passes through
But not shape
Rough edges made smooth
No longer cutting
Water worn
Tamed

Life fragment
Tossed overboard
Scraping the bottom
An accident of time and tide

Fall, 1996

MANGO! MON-GO!

*If there really is a Garden of Eden, and if people enjoy its fruit,
then the mango certainly holds a place of honor.*

from an Israeli newspaper,
translated from the Hebrew

Mango! Mango!
Mongo in Hebrew
Go, mon, go!

Through the gateway for beginners
To an El-Al high
Then a Tel Aviv low
Where a hand is a *yod*
And a foot is a *regel*
But despite all that
A bagel's still a bagel.

You know bagel
And I know bagel

And Einstein gave us MC^2
But did he know *regel*
Like I know *regel*?
To tell the truth
I doubt he even cared.

July, 2005

ROCK, SCISSORS, PAPER

Rock, scissors, paper:
Rock breaks scissors,
Scissors cuts paper,
Paper covers rock.

Fist, fingers, palm:
Fist breaks fingers,
Fingers cut palm,
Palm covers fist.

Red, blue, yellow:
Red breaks blue,
Blue cuts yellow,
Yellow covers red.

Orange, green, purple:
Orange bleeds yellow,
Green bleeds blue,
Purple bleeds red.

Blood, sweat, tears:
Blood breaks sweat,
Sweat cuts tears,
Tears covers blood.

Blood, sweat, tears:
Blood salts sweat,
Sweat salts tears,
Tears salt blood.

Rock, scissors, paper:
Rock breaks scissors,
Scissors cuts paper,
Paper covers rock.

May, 2009

THE FROG AT RITTENHOUSE SQUARE

The frog at Rittenhouse Square faces forever East—
Where the sun rises over the spires and the aspirations
                    of downtown Philadelphia—
Because the sculptor who had made him happened to put him there,
Forever fixed in that position, formulated in stone,
Squatting upon a stone pedestal,
Low enough for the very young to mount in an ecstasy of innocence,
Large enough to light up their eyes
In celebration of the unchained exuberance of childhood.

The frog seems so comfortable right where he is—
As if a frog with a heart of stone could choose otherwise—
Here in the center of the park in the center of the city,
Within hopping distance of the bubbling fountain
Whose living waters he can never drink—
Like the Attic Lover on that ancient Grecian urn
Who can never drink the living waters of his dreams.

The frog's bulging eyes first meet mine
On a July morning, already steaming though not yet nine,
Still a splash of puddles leftover from yesterday's downpours;
And I imagine him in the dress of other seasons:
A thin blanket of October leaves covering his dew damp skin,
A Joseph frog in a coat of many colors;
A far thicker blanket of January snow,
The surprise of a deep drift burying all but the stony eyes atop his head;
The melt of spring, park lights creating in the soft fog of an April evening
The illusion of a gauzy veil upon his soft-edged form.

The frog at Rittenhouse Square faces forever East
Towards the dawning of the new day,
Calling his children to climb up and play,
The anguish of the dying sun forever behind him.

July, 2008

SEASON OF GHOSTS AND MISTS

It was evening all afternoon.
It was snowing
And it was going to snow.

Wallace Stevens, "Thirteen Ways of
of Looking at a Blackbird"

Season of ghosts and mists,
Pumpkins and puddings,
Sun-dried leaves crackling into an allspice
Of apple, squash, plum, and pear,
Blue sky symphonies of cloudless delight
Called earlier and earlier
Into the deepening chill of nutmeg night.

A turn of the wind and then,
And then the rain, the loud pouring rain
Rousing the snoring ghosts of all our yesterdays,
Driving the leaves, now brittle and brown,
Down, down, down low
Into afternoons that are all evening
When it is snowing and going to snow.

October, 2008

THAT "FOUL RAG-AND-BONE SHOP"

I must lie down where all the ladders start
In the foul rag-and-bone shop of the heart.

W. B. Yeats, The Circus Animals' Desertion

Words are the problem with poetry,
Words the solution, but only in part:
Magistrates of meaning, policemen of paradox, tyrants of time,
Words govern the ungovernable, bring structure to no-structure,
Create and carry a clarifying consciousness
Through chaotic everflow riverrun yes and no
Jumbled up tomorrow yesterday today.

Oh, the seductive allure of verbs
And the adverbs who render them
              sometimes slippery, sometimes bold and brash,
Like the strong and definitive nouns they call to action,
And all those well-dressed adjectives
Back to back in do-sa-do with proper and improper nouns
On whose muscular necks hang Western bolo ties,
A square dance of joyful cacophony,
And the propositions of one hundred wayward prepositions,
And the necessary grief of copulatives and conjunctions
Leading to conjunctions, and, alas, at times to disjunctions
That our fool flesh is heir to . . .

Oh you words, you circus animals of my imagination,
My imperfect tools, do not forsake me, oh my darlings;
Do not seclude yourselves in some cobweb-ridden
Foul language rag-and-bone shop,
Sterile sign tacked to locked door:
CLOSED FOR INVENTORY.

I turn to You, Erato, Poet Part of God.
When You hear me knocking, don't say I can't come in.
Give me Your gift of words, whatever words You have,
Be they blunted, broken, a bunch of barbaric yawps.
I need them to pierce the sacred mysteries of a child's
                    Yes I can!
And the foul rag-and-bone shop of an old man's heart.

                              June, 2008

IV

I am waiting for my train to come in.

TRAIN STATION, PROVIDENCE

I am waiting for my case to come up
and I am waiting
for a rebirth of wonder . . .

Lawrence Ferlinghetti,
I AM WAITING

I am waiting for my train to come in.
I am waiting for my train to carry me off
To the big beat dynamo of the Big Apple,
Where I will wait for a fresh wordburst
From poet's mouth to infuse my dried up soul
With the rebirth of wonder.

I am waiting without my baggage,
I am waiting with all my baggage,
I am waiting for my train to come in.

I am waiting inside the station.
I am wondering, wrapped in winter coat,
How the windy breath of January
Has found her way into this marble void
Under a cold and faceless dome.

I am waiting for my train to come in.
I am waiting for my time to be neither wrong nor right.
I am waiting for the rebirth of wonder.

May, 2008

FACING MYSELF

Cry 'Havoc!' The beach is NOT taken.
The beach is NOT taken.
And let slip the dogs of war.
Early morning. Omaha Beach is
Not taken.

Ricocheting bullets flying helter-skelter
All the pots and pans of Hell's kitchen rattling and clattering
Terror raining down from impregnable German pill boxes
Bodies shredded in bloody sand, lifeless heaps of smelly entrails
Language helpless in chaotic din.

Here I stand 63 years after the fact
In front of the bathroom mirror
A graybeard in need of a shave
Staring at the wrinkling face
That wasn't there then,
That couldn't have been there:
Three weeks to go in mother's womb.

Had I been my father
I could have been there;
He was the right age,
But his daughter,
Another one on the way,
And his job kept him at home,
Away from the gore.

I look in the mirror
And see my father at 63;
And if I look more carefully,
I see my father's father as well.
They say I am his *spitting image.*
And I see my son David
Staring back at me from the future.
He has long since worn my face.

Faces in the mirror,
Faces that have never faced the sting of battle,
Eyes that have never witnessed the fall of a friend,
Ears that have never heard *bombs bursting in air*
Noses that have never breathed the stench of rotting flesh,
Mouths that have never encouraged comrades in arms.

I move the razor across my cheek one last time
And wonder why I wasn't there then
And why it is that my granddaughter
Happened to be born on D-Day.

November, 2007

IN THE KITCHEN OF ALZHEIMER'S

Weak rapping on the bedroom door
Like the sound of a small bird tapping
High-pitched voice squeaking out of the throat
Of the woman who used to be my mother
Jim! Jim! Come quickly!

Kitchen—a Walt Disney scene from *The Sorcerer's Apprentice*
Awash with water from the overflowing sink
Plastic plate mistaken for a slice of bread
Melted forever into the toaster oven
Now drowned, useless, beyond repair

Like the old woman
Who put it in the bottom of the sink
Never again to rise to the surface

                                        Summer, 2003

A POEM ADDRESSED TO YOU

Adonai natan, v'Adonai lakakh . . .
Adonai has given,
and Adonai has taken away . . .
Job 1.21

Oh, the day that Edith, eyes blank as snow,
Hooted broken bird-song sounds
That snapped forever the twisted cord
Binding mother to son:
Who-are-you?

Where were You
When my father phoned me on his long night of hopelessness?
She thinks I'm an impostor. What can I do?
How language hangs helpless. Mother drowning
In a sea of words. What can I do?
What can I do?

Were You with me in the nursing home?
Were You there? Mother undressing, garment by garment,
Crazy cacophony of ancient eating sounds
Sucking me into a black hole of helpless humiliation.
Mother spilling sentence fragments
Like pieces of an unsolved jigsaw.
Mother, let me stay a half an hour more,
Let me put your life together again,
Piece by piece.

Hear the rain-damp clumps of April clay
Thump-thumping on the casket,
Ghost sounds linking past and future.
Flowing teenage tears, my son's tears—
I command him with my eyes:
One day, David, you will do this for me,
Shovelful by shovelful.

O Devouring Presence,
You have taken away, and You have given back again.
Open now the graves of memory and of hope
And breathe Your Weary Self into these weary bones!

        Summer, 1994

MOTHER

In your death
You wear blue overalls,
A gray slicker,
And hip boots of camouflage green.
Armed with shovel and hose,
You trudge into the elephant house
To begin your nightly work.
Haloed be thy eve.

The visitors are gone.
You are alone
With the two of them
And pile upon pile of their half-dried dung.
Shovel and hose, shovel and hose
Shovel shovel hose hose . . .

Down now on your knees,
You remove a red toothbrush
From a pocket in your overalls.
Dipping the tiny nest of bristles
Into a bucket of bleach,
You begin at the far corner
And scrub and scrub scrub
The expanding patch of gray concrete
Until sunrise.

                                        Summer, 1999

The line in italics in from *Finnegans Wake*
                by James Joyce

GROUND ZERO

The fence is tall and green.
I do not know if I have arrived.
Up sixteen steps to gain perspective
On what is no longer here:
Absence of love, absence of malice,
Absence of absence. Numbing nullity
In the lengthening shadows of a December afternoon,
A hole in the heart of New York City

Like the hole in my heart after mother died
Not quite a year before her death—
Shutting the door to her second-floor apartment for the last time,
Stunning straw hat, ringed with red ribbon, crowning her white hair—
Expression blank except for a hint of confusion—
Climbing down the sixteen steps towards extinction
                in a nursing home;

Like the hole in my heart that would begin to close
Only after I could admit that that woman
Climbing down those sixteen steps
Without mind, without memory, without ability
To connect one sentence to another—

Only after I could finally say that that woman
Climbing down those sixteen steps
Used to be

        My mother.

                                    Summer, 2004

INTIMATIONS OF MORTALITY

I.   *A LONG SUMMER EVENING*

So hard to see the subtle shades
Of backyard hydrangeas in the lingering light
As the green fullness of the long July day fades

Into the summer softness of the welcoming night—
Ghosts flying freely, shadows of bat wings,
The mosquito-filled air holding not quite

The hum of happiness, the ripe promise that sings
In the heart and beats in the head
That hope of "forever" which this season brings

To a long summer evening
            where sometimes there sleeps
                    a devouring dread.

II.   *HER EYES*

Her eyes are my sister's eyes,
Unfocused, on the verge of tears,
Eyes that hold a world of sighs

Unexpressed during the chain of years,
Eyes which gaze into the middle distance,
Eyes which see beyond all hope, beyond all fears.

In her gloved hands, the full fragrance
Of a burgeoning bouquet, a flowering breath;
And on her head a flowered hat—in gentle defiance

Of the call of tomorrow, the call of death.

December, 2008

NO ALARM CLOCK NOW

The pure pleasure of awakening unalarmed
To the call of my body's secret rhythms,
Freed from the bondage of other people's woes.

No apologies for measuring my mornings in coffee spoons;
My cup runneth over onto the pages of the day's news—
                Jackson Pollack dribbles.
I take delight as the latest stain spreads out
                like a dark brown amoeba
Upon the words of an unrepentant columnist,
Blotting them out along with his sour views,
Which in recent weeks have pushed me towards indigestion.

I smile a polite thank-you to the rising sun
While savoring the soft cheese
In the omelet of a new day.

                        June, 2008

EBBTIDE

The tide of life, once flood, has turned to ebb,
The sound of soft waves sliding off the sand.
The spider ties up memories in her web;
The rusty clock still jerks her tired hand.

The moon, once friend, has fled from my night sky,
Withholding now the comfort of her light.
All hope suspended, although no fear to die;
The bats, the bats within me are in flight.

My dreams of life renewed begin to flower:
Half a prayer takes shape upon my lips;
The other half, my soul it does devour,
For I know full well the sun is in eclipse.

The receding tide no turn of chance can bring,
As I'm done in by too much sad remembering.

                                April, 2008

AUTUMN TWILIGHT EMBERS

translation of Sonnet 73 by William Shakespeare

I have reached the autumn of my life.
Brittle leaves, yellowed and few, still cling
To bone bare branches shaking in the cold
And whistling winds. No bird song now. No, never.

My day is dragging into dying light,
My sun sinking in the western sky,
As I await the coming of the night,
The sleep from which no earthbound soul awakens.

Reduced am I to autumn twilight embers
Which sit upon the ashes of my dreams.
The overreaching of hot-blood youth
Has consumed me—body, hope, desire.

      You knew me then, you see me now, you love me still—
      That is all I know and all I need to know.

              May, 1996

THIRTY MINUTES BEFORE I DIE:

musings for Selichot evening, 5765

So this is IT:
Cup almost empty
Sand passed through
The neck of the hour glass
A strange, curious calm
Buber calls IT
The onset of nothingness
If IT is nothing, then there is nothing
I can do about IT

Time of infinite resignation
Time to stop fighting
Time to say *Thank you, God,*
For most this amazing day!
Mother, father, brother, sister
Wife, daughter, son, son-in-law, daughter-in-law . . .

And for you, my children's children,
My cup runneth over
With a heart full of gladness I spill out my old life
To make room for your new lives,
New hopes, new dreams, new loves . . .

Shema Yisrael Adonai Eloheynu Adonai Echad

September 24, 2005

THERE MUST BE PIZZA AFTER DEATH

There must be pizza after death:
What shall I fear?
Slice upon slice awaits my afterlife,
Each piled high with my corpse's delight:
Five fatty cheeses
Four oily veggies
Three smoking sausages
Two squishy fishes
But no partridge
In heaven's pantry.

                              Summer, 2004

THE RETURN OF GRANDPA PAUL

The memory of Grandpa Paul,
Like acid on a copper plate,
Etches deep lines on what I have chosen to forget.
The boulders blocking entrance
To the cave of years gone by
Are rolled away, having no more power
To hold me hostage to this day;

Now I too am a grandfather—three times over.
What might it mean to say
That nothing else has changed?

And now the past will be at least
Slightly more than past—
Though hardly completely present,
The present being a sliding slip knot
Binding time elapsed with time that's yet to come,
The present being fragile fragments
Flying towards tomorrow in search of a way
To heal the wounds of yesterday.

And now, again alive, that flash of Grandpa's anger,
That lash of tongue to chide my younger brother
For his blatant disrespect,
Though he was not more than five
And grandpa three score and ten:

When you grow up, little boy,
You'll be ashamed of what you said.

When I grow up, grandpa,
You'll be dead.

February, 2009

KAFKA'S HUNGER ARTIST

In the beginning Kafka's Hunger Artist
Drew large crowds to the cage
Where he sat cross-legged on his bed of straw,
A living impersonation of a dying animal.

But all too soon the crowd lost interest
In the non-spectacle of one lonely man
Slowly starving himself into a bag of bones.

You could hear the cry of collective relief
When what was left of the man was replaced
By a living, robust, roaring tiger.

April, 2009

PAIR OF SHOES

Voiceless in the closet
Dust thick on cracked leather skin
Tongues curled and ugly
As a Dali painting. Sightless eyes
Stretched shapeless by laces
Too knotted up to bind
Or to release

                              Summer, 1999

FINAL JOURNEY

> *. . . v'hasneh ainehnu ukahl.*
> *. . . and the bush is not consumed.*
> *Exodus 3.2*

I crawl up the grassy hill on all fours,
Bleached by the sun,
Tail between my tired legs.

My goal is not a shingled house,
Shuttered and secure,
But a spare fence of wire and wood
Defining the boundary between what is
And what is yet to be.

I drag myself in midday heat,
Too old to sweat.
The fence recedes like the horizon
On a summer blue sea.

Right paw, left paw,
Right paw, left . . .

Time contracts into Eternal Now
As I dissolve into the Womb of Light.
The fence is all ablaze,
But the fence is not consumed.

January, 1988

YOU IN THE SPRINGTIME

You in the springtime of your lives
So energy burst young
Who thrill at the living edge of ocean blue
Dreaming of endless sand and surf

You too will stop riding the waves
Up and down down and up and up
Even you will lie down in winter
And die

Autumn, 2006

FATHER

Maine woods, August, 1997

An old man limps up steep stairs
Linking a rocky lake shore
To a cabin in the pines.
His right hand grabs a crude wooden rail,
Pulling himself higher and higher,
One step at a time.
He does not complain.
In his left hand hangs
A fish stringer from which dangle
Two large bass, freshly killed.

A day or two later,
After a morning on the water,
The old man tumbles
Out of a small boat
Onto a rickety dock.
He remains on hands and knees,
Gasping for air.
I kneel down to help him to his feet.
Pouring his eyes into my face,
He says: *Don't be angry.*
This is who I am now.

December, 1999

SAILING FROM BYZANTIUM

That is no country for old men. The young
In one another's arms, birds in the trees . . .
The salmon-falls, the mackerel-crowded seas . . .

William Butler Yeats, Sailing to Byzantium

I.   A Country for Old Men

This is a country for old men—
No young in one another's arms,
No mackerel-crowded seas
Nor artifice of eternity—
Just the still, sad signs
Of rock hard mortality:

Two abandoned crutches, a solitary wheelchair
Keeping silent watch over a deserted pool table,
Its green felt unscarred by use.
And over there on a quiet shelf,
Etched on a silver bowl for all to see,
A list of names and dates,
Best bridge players in the place;
And on top of that list
In that almost empty room
Stands the name of my father.

II.   Dinner at Five

The dining room is almost full.
He lowers himself from walker to chair,
Stares at the man who stares
Back across the foodless table.

A woman last week complained of his dribble:
One part spilled soup, one part father's spittle;
So now he occupies an exile's space,
Nothing to say, unaware of his place.
And for your main course you want?
And for your main course you want?
The waitress persists, but my father is silent—
Can not remember and can not hear.

III.   On the Phone

I'm dead! he tells me.
I won't eat or drink,
I won't take my pills,
And I won't use that glove
To scoop out my rock hard turds.

Don't try to stop me;
I DECLARE MYSELF DEAD!

———

"We found him in the closet
With a belt around his neck."

———

Why shouldn't I?

Against the law . . .

. . . and I love you, Dad.
Do you love me?

IV.   When He Was Still God

We sit side by side on the synagogue bench,
Dressed in our dark Yom Kippur suits.
He tells me: "I say *Yizkor** for my father."
My father's father, the Jacob I have never seen;
But they see in me his "spitting image"
Though I am not yet a teen.

A dark cloud covers me, my body chills:
My father, my God will abandon me one day,
As I abandon him to rush outside to play
Beneath the sad smile of the September sun.

* *Yizkor* is a Hebrew prayer said in memory of the dead.

V.   The Open Window

The tired wreck of my father's body
Lies sprawled upon the double bed
He brought with him to his final home.
In the proud presence of sons and grandsons
He offers this confession:
I am sorry. I was wrong
To want to give this up,
Wrong to want to leave you.
But tell me, am I really here?
Or is this all a dream?

The June breeze pours her cleansing breath
Into the stale sickness of his room.
The Jamaican health aide heads down the hall,
Having opened the window
And raised the blinds
To let in the air,
To welcome the light.

Father's Day, 2002

SELF-PORTRAIT

His hair is thinning but there,
More white than gray.
The wrinkles on his face, not yet deep,
Convey the passage of years;
But his blue eyes still sparkle
With youthful enthusiasms.

His body moves with no trace of grace,
Even clumsily, but with energy,
Not unlike a playful bear.
He wears his awkwardness with nonchalance,
As if to say:
God gave me these feet, these knees, these hips
To carry me on my journey.

Summer, 1998

WHAT REMAINS?

reflections upon a passage in
Abigail Thomas, A Three Dog Life,
2007

And after the storm has subsided,
And after her husband has lost his mind,
After the skid, the midnight lamppost,
The fog and the ice, the moment's inattention,
She poses a question, a question to herself:
What one thing in my life remains stable?

And she turns to you, and she turns to me:
Tell me, she says, *I am taking a poll.*
What one thing in your life remains stable?

And what is there to say?
After all of our comings and all of our goings,
Our fallings and failures, our dejections and resurrections—
After our parents have left us and our children have fled us,
And our work has so tired us that our work has retired us,
What is there to say? Tell me, what is there to say?

August, 2007

TO JOHN COLTRANE

"He never stopped surprising himself."
Alice Coltrane to Nat Hentoff
regarding her late husband

Ra-ta-tat-tat of October storm surprises the night,
Lively accompaniment to an Atlantic label LP:

Coltrane's magic horn hitting the highs, the lows, the in-betweens
Transforming Oscar's lightweight lyrics, *raindrops on roses,*
Whiskers on kittens, into John's fiery imperatives—
The cry, the shout, the soaring prayer without words . . .

Rhythm, rhythm! Nothing less, *nothing less*, says Nat,
Than a brave new universe of sound and feeling.

On the kitchen table, record cover, 1961:
John stands proud and black and thirty-five.
A slight forward tilt of neck and shoulders,
Lips kissing in music love the mouth of his soprano sax,
Caressed into an ecstasy never before felt
By man or by woman.

At the piano the giant hands of McCoy Tyner stretching,
Stretching far beyond the octave, forming,
Forming impossible chords, inverting,
Inventing out of the depths of E-minor ninth—
Subtle, insistent pulse: Elvin Jones on drums, Steve Davis on bass . . .

Let your sax sound at my funeral, John, let your soul-song
Search for the next surprise.
Carry me, carry me with you into eternity!

October, 2009

WHAT MATTERS

Motes of dust swimming in a sunbeam
The sound of the tide licking smooth stones
Pine trees reflecting deep green
Upon the rippleless surface of a lake in Maine—
Loons yodeling and crying, crashing and splashing
The moist hot hug of August, January's icy embrace
City streets dancing in winter light of late afternoon
Sky scraping buildings casting giant shadows

Pumpkins! Pumpkins! Pumpkins piled high
Decked out in unrhymed orange against the October sky
Pumpkins for square-toothed jack-o'-lanterns—
Candle-lit smiles on Halloween stoops
Pumpkins for the taste of Thanksgiving
For the taste of family, their dishes dreaming
In the unwashed truth of a kitchen sink

A two-day growth of beard reflected in a morning mirror
The look of your eyes! The look of her eyes!
The look of his eyes! The look of your eyes!
A key turning in the door at the end of day

The jazzy cacophony of ten thousand madly joyful voices
Without rhyme, without reason
Singing praises to the One,
Singing praises to yes, You, *Ya!*
Hallelu Ya! Hallelu Ya!

                                    January, 2008

A GLUM NOVEMBER DAY

> *Dor holech, v'dor bah . . .*
> *A generation goes,*
> *and a generation comes . . .*
> —*Ecclesiastes 1.4*

It was a glum November day,
The Sunday afternoon just before
Or Just after Thanksgiving.
I do not remember.
I was ten years old, perhaps eleven.
I can't be sure.
The air was cold and damp,
Dark sky spitting snow and sleet,
Flakes and pellets melting upon hitting the ground.

I am always sad when the snow fails to stick,
As if Nature is leaving her work undone.

Then we were five:
Mother, father, older sister, younger brother,
And I, securely in the middle, cocooned,
Protected in a pine green jacket,
Untouched by the outside.
Brief trip to the country, to the Watchungs,
(They call them mountains in New Jersey)
To see the dull brown oak leaves hanging on
In indefinite afterlife—
Many branches already bare,
All song long since silenced,
Though no hint of ruin,
Not then.

My father took great joy in that day's darkness,
For the gloomy weather was a sign, a vindication
Of his power in middle age to solve problems still.
That very morning on the puzzle page of *The New York Times*
He had cracked the code of a Kingsley Double-Crostic,
Whose message, having taken shape letter by letter,
Word by word, began:
"It was a glum November day . . ."

That was then,
Fifty years ago or so.
Today my mother is no more—Alzheimer's
My father is no more—heart disease.
My sister is no more—cancer.
Today, a glum November day,
A day dripping with cold November rain.

But now, towards evening, the sun smiles through the clouds,
And I am greeted with the laughter of my two granddaughters.

November, 2007

Edwards Brothers,Inc!
Thorofare, NJ 08086
13 April, 2011
BA2011103